WHO
AM
I
LISA COLASO

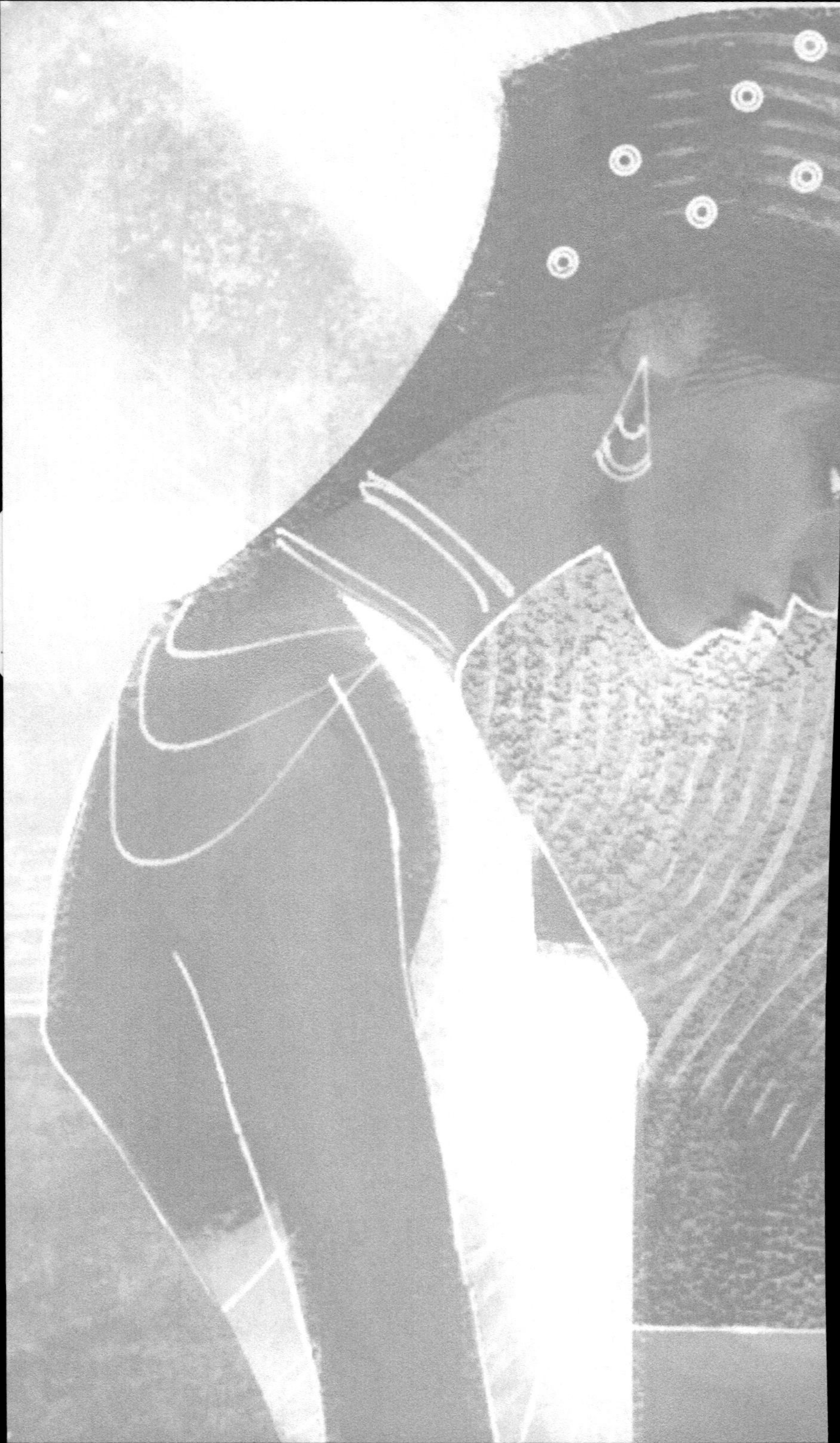

WHO AM I

11 WAYS TO UNBECOMING AND DISCOVERING YOUR AUTHENTIC SELF

Clever Fox® PUBLISHING
Chennai • Bangalore

LISA COLASO

CLEVER FOX PUBLISHING
Chennai, India

Published by CLEVER FOX PUBLISHING 2025

ISBN: 978-93-6707-933-1

DEDICATION

To Lester, my spouse, my partner, my friend,
—my greatest teacher in this lifetime. He showed me how to be myself without worrying about others' opinions of me, amongst so many other lessons and for that, I am truly grateful.
In May 2023, he sat across the table from me ensuring I could write this book without distraction, lending his support by dealing with the mundane.
Sadly Lester transitioned in April 2024 and is missed deeply.

To Liam and Simone,
my children who inspire me to be a better version of myself every day and believe in me more than I believe in myself.

To my Dad,
who nurtured my love for reading in every way possible; his encouragement has helped me become an author today. I am forever thankful.

To my Mum,
who expressed her talents in every way. She inspired me to explore my own and gave me wings to fly. Your love and support in all things are invaluable to me.

ACKNOWLEDGEMENTS

Deep gratitude and appreciation to my dearest Friends

Preethi Mahadeviah
who patiently edited this book multiple times and provided invaluable insights on writing more effectively. Thank you ever so much!

Priya Mendens
who crafted the beautiful design, and layout of this book.
(with the help of art from various artists sourced online ~ I thank all you doodlers).
I am deeply grateful for your unconditional desire to help and support me in healing the world.

Jatin Gupta
@inspiringjatin, whose course on writing a book was instrumental in helping me commit to and complete this project.
Thank you Jatin Gupta!

Rebecca Helmsley
@beckyhelmsleypoetry for giving me permission to use her beautiful poem "Breathe" in this book. Thank you!

To all my mentors, teachers,
from whom I have learnt through various courses, books, stimulating and thought-provoking interactions, I am grateful to you for sharing your knowledge and wisdom with me.

And to all the friends and well-wishers
Thank You
for your unwavering support and encouragement.
Your belief in me, means so much.

To my Divine Team, Angels, Guides, Masters and Loved Ones,
thank you for your guidance and protection at all times.

THE PREFACE

The purpose of this book is to bring awareness to you. The awareness that life can be different and that you can liberate yourself from your limiting beliefs and social conditioning and be the best version of who you choose to be.

I have studied counselling and various modalities in healing, and I realised that not everyone would be open to seeing a therapist. I have to say that more people are open today than they were a decade ago.

I grew up always having an instinct for understanding far beyond my years. Which often led, to me being told I was 'too big for my boots' when I showed maturity that surprised others, and when I acted my age, I was told to 'grow up'. I always felt I never belonged. I couldn't always relate to my peers and older kids didn't always want my company. I learnt to treasure my own company. I became an avid reader, found my passion in baking and could keep myself occupied for vast amounts of time. I had friends and when I did hang out, I enjoyed my time with them.

I spent a lot of my time, observing and studying people, probably because of the mandate laid down by my father, "Children are to be seen and not heard." and "Keep your eyes and ears wide open and your mouth shut." Well, I suppose it did serve me some good but also gave me a thyroid issue, which comes from blockage of the throat chakra due to "lack of expression."

I found my tribe in college and parts of myself, and as a young employee, I became quite the confidant, successful young adult, who did well for herself. I was a go-getter with dreams... until the conditioning kicked in.

In India, girls are groomed to be married-off sooner than later; and that ends their parent's responsibility, until they start pressurising you for grand kids. Marriage and parenting to me became the most challenging tasks in my life. I was no more responsible for myself and my needs, and began to lose myself in the whole process of being responsible for the lives of my children that I was given to guide into this world. I started to feel torn between what I felt and what I had been told to be; and that accelerated my journey deeper into self-discovery through reading, studying, therapy and with putting all that I had learnt, into practise to become who I wanted to be.

As I edged towards my forties, I found myself playing several roles as a mother, wife, daughter, friend, and more. I was spending less time being myself and felt stretched and fragmented. Along with this, came a lot of dissatisfaction, insecurity, low self-confidence and guilt. The guilt was because I was stretched so thin between all the roles, I didn't even think I was good at any. Most importantly, I didn't have time for myself, to even explore who I was anymore. This dissatisfaction and guilt led me to introspect and one day I just decided to drop the guilt. It felt too big a burden to carry, especially being the perfectionist that I was. The first thing I did which was the hardest, was that I learned to say no!!! I am helpful by nature and could never say no to others. And oftentimes, found myself being used and taken advantage of. I was certainly aware of this and it annoyed me, that I let it happen every time.

At the start, I kept justifying to myself all the reasons I needed to say no. Till eventually, I realized I didn't need to justify anymore. This was one of the most liberating things I did.

I learned to accept myself, warts and all. I learned to appreciate myself and all that I did and was capable of. I learned to stop worrying about what others would think of me and decided to be unapologetically me, irrespective of what others thought. I stopped people-pleasing.

As I let go of old stereotyped patterns and behaviours that were intricately woven into the old me, I spent more time on and for myself. I am still helpful and still play these roles, but on my terms and how I choose to! I now draw boundaries of what is acceptable and not.

In this book, I share the steps I learnt from all the various modalities I have learnt, the self-help books I've read and used on myself to create a path of unfolding and unbecoming. This unbecoming lead me to find my true authentic self and purpose. I learnt to love and appreciate myself for all that I am. I am and will always be a work in progress and a lifelong learner, where at times, I need to realign myself when I catch myself getting stuck in a problem. These tools are here to help you as much as they did me. The process has not always been easy however it has been extremely liberating and absolutely reassuring to see how far I have come. Let me just say, I am at peace with where I am and with who I am today. It gives me immense pleasure and purpose to share these tools with you so that you feel that liberation and freedom to accept and be your unique self.

LISA COLASO

Contents

Section 1

Lisa Colaso

SECTION 2

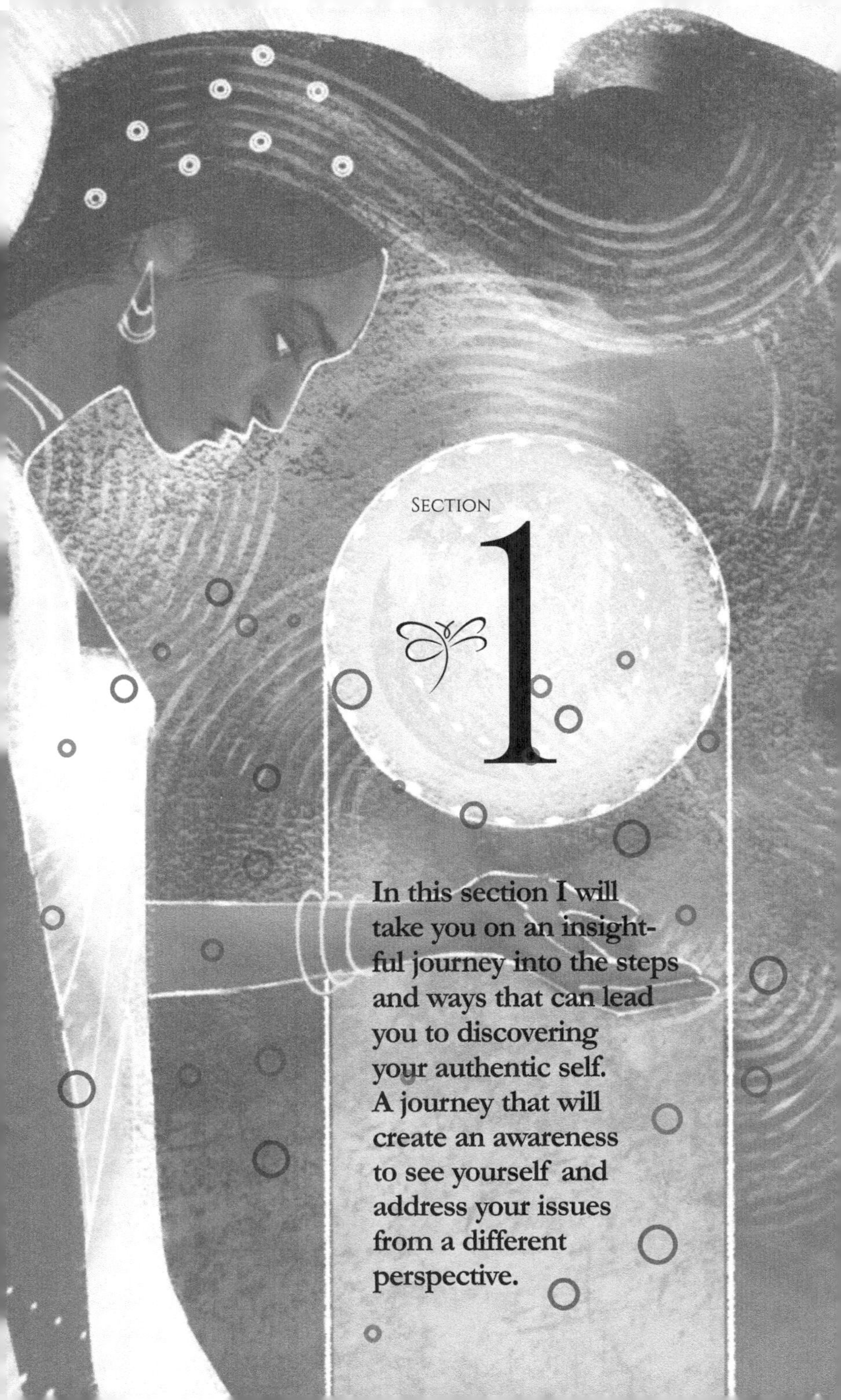

Section 1

In this section I will take you on an insightful journey into the steps and ways that can lead you to discovering your authentic self. A journey that will create an awareness to see yourself and address your issues from a different perspective.

CHAPTER 1

WHAT IS AUTHENTICITY?

And the dandelion does not stop growing
because it is told it is a weed.
The dandelion does not care what others see.
It says, One day they will be making wishes upon me.

B. Atkinson

WHAT IS AUTHENTICITY?

Authenticity means being true to yourself in thought, word, and deed. It means that what you say aligns with what you do. Your authentic self goes way beyond what you do professionally, the possessions, wealth, status you acquire, or the roles you play. It is about who you are at your core, reflected in your external being.

Authenticity is about integrity and honesty about everything that you are and owning it.

What is the value of knowing and living from your authentic self?

Every-one, is born with unique gifts and talents. We are all born to shine. Somehow in our childhood, we were all subjected to a fair amount of conditioning, fears, and beliefs passed on to us by our families and it can carry on for generations. In this process, we forget who we are and are taught to conform to these beliefs, familial and societal conditioning, just to be accepted. As we grow into adulthood, we often make choices based on our conditioned beliefs to please our families and society. As a result, we end up living a life that others dictate. We want to fit into a life that is acceptable in society.

What does it mean to be your authentic self?

Being your authentic self means being in the flow. To reconnect with the deepest part of yourself: your core. At your core, you know who you are and how you can live the best version of who you were born to be. When you are at your core, you embrace your unique qualities, traits, and talents, rather than fitting into a stereotype that ticks all the boxes.

'AUTHENTICITY IS A COLLECTION OF
CHOICES THAT WE MAKE EVERY DAY.
IT IS ABOUT THE CHOICE TO SHOW UP
AND BE REAL. THE CHOICE, TO BE HONEST.
THE CHOICE TO LET OUR TRUE SELVES BE SEEN.'
~ BRENE BROWN.

How do I know when I am not authentic?

When you are not being authentic, you live a life where you always feel compelled to show your best version. You play roles of having the perfect image, being the perfect host, the perfect son/daughter, the ideal spouse, the perfect parent, and so on. You are constantly walking a tightrope, putting on a show, and leading a stressful life. Living a life like this causes you to suppress your emotions, your anxiety, and the less agreeable attributes of yourself to conform with what society dictates of how you should be.

You wear a mask to fit in or act in a way that others think you should. When you ignore your beliefs and values just to fit in, you become upset with yourself and even feel remorse, shame, and guilt. That is a good time to ask yourself what being true to your inner self means.

> *Let me share a personal story here of my journey with baking and cooking.*
>
> As a young child, perhaps even a toddler, I never really played with dolls or stuffed toys, even though I received them as gifts. I always remember playing with kitchen sets and cooking make-believe food. When I turned seven, I decided to learn how to bake. My mother was a fantastic cook and baker who encouraged me to learn and taught me the baking basics. The only two things I was not allowed to touch at that age were the oven and the electric beaters, so I had to call her to help me use them, put the trays into the oven, and remove them when done. So, every Saturday, I would bake and try out new recipes for cakes, cookies, and other desserts. In those days, in the early 80s in India, cocoa was an expensive commodity, and one relied on relatives abroad to bring them the good stuff. Being a rookie baker, I was not allowed to use it. Such things were reserved for the pro, my mother. So I often used Drinking chocolate, a poor substitute. You can only imagine the outcome! And, of course, being a novice baker, I would have more misses than hits when I baked. The flops made me and my baking the butt of my older brothers' jokes. I am sure you all have siblings who have been in either

position and can relate to how siblings rib each other. But I didn't close shop and run away from it all. Instead, I persisted, believing I would be great at it one day, and kept at it despite the relentless teasing I had to endure. I often ate all the flops myself to prove it wasn't so bad, and they would laugh at me even more. It taught me to develop my palate and figure out how to do it better the next time. Nothing deterred me. Now, I have had a business as a caterer, baker, cake artist, teacher, and instructor for almost 30 years! I have earned a reputation in the food circles in Bangalore and Dubai, where I lived for a while.

I am ever so grateful that, at the time, I honoured my inner voice and passion for keeping at it because the hard work and determination paid off.

You have all encountered similar situations that might have shut down your passions. The only way to silence the critics is to honour your dreams, follow them no matter what, and come out on top!

When you let go of your fears and your borrowed beliefs that you are not good enough or inadequate, it is only then that you awaken your inner voice and unleash the power and potential within you to shine your inner light. We all have more power than we realize: the power to make a difference. That is when you are being true to yourself.

YOU KNOW YOU ARE BEING AUTHENTIC WHEN...

You are confident to share your opinions and ideas healthily.

You make decisions that align with your values and beliefs.

You pursue your passions.

You set boundaries and stand up for yourself.

You walk away from toxic behaviours.

You move past being a victim and find your inner power.

You learn to say NO!

You can speak your truth.

You stop caring about what others think or say about you.

You have empathy and compassion for yourself and others.

You can accept your missteps and learn from them.

You accept all parts of yourself without shame or guilt.

You forgive and let go of past pain and old wounds.

You stop being a people pleaser.

You become emotionally mature.

You have a healthy ego.

You feel secure and at peace with who you are.

You listen to your inner voice, your intuition.

The decisions you make are in favour of honouring and respecting yourself.

CHAPTER 2

PERCEPTIONS

Perception moulds, shapes, and influences our experience of our personal reality.

Linda Humphreys
a psychologist and coach

WHAT IS PERCEPTION?

Our perception is how we view the world based on the sum total of our experiences and the influences that dominate how we perceive the world.

They influence the direction of our focus and how we process, recall, decode, and understand to make decisions and take action. Therefore, our perceptions represent what reality is to us.

Some may have a negative view of themselves and the world even if they have a good life. They seem focussed on all the things that are not going well instead of the good in their lives. And some may not have much material wealth or be in crappy situations, but they will still find a way to look at all the good in their lives and make the most of it. And some find humour in any situation.

Our perception gives us insight into who we are and how we view the world through our responses to others, events, and situations. It can teach us much about ourselves and how we react or respond, whether fear-based, negative, positive, or grateful for what is.

Do people all have the same perception?

No two people have the same perception. We may have similar perceptions based on shared experiences, upbringing, or religious beliefs. Siblings in the same household can have vastly different perceptions of life because their perceptions reflect their own feelings, thoughts, and experiences. We also argue when we have opposing points of view, and one tries to convince the other of theirs. This happens as the ego comes into play, wanting to be right. But if we step back and realise that each person has their own perception and truths, we become more accepting of the situation and realise we do not need to convince people that they were wrong and we were right. Everyone has a right to their own perception based on what feels real to them.

What contributes to our perceptions?

Our upbringing, religious and cultural beliefs, education, sensory experiences, media, values, and past experiences influence our perceptions. All these influences lay the groundwork for us to pay heed to specific information and to understand and collate that information in particular ways.

An individual's personality influences how they process information and determine their perceptions.

People are more driven to respond to stimuli that have previously benefited them or to meet a more pressing need in a specific scenario.

Patterns learned from previous perceptions also influence how people assign meaning and act on those perceptions.

Let me give you a more typical example of perceptions. You have all heard or even used the simile, "As proud as a peacock." And I'm sure you will agree that it has a negative connotation when used. For some reason, peacocks caught my curiosity a couple of years ago. I have always admired their beauty. This time it got me thinking about this line with such a negative reference to peacocks. Now imagine the weight of its plumage and how heavy a load it must carry. Imagine if we were to bear that weight, day in and day out? And then it can still put on such a beautiful display and dance to court a female and show its beauty all around. Why shouldn't it be proud? I am sure we all have peacock moments that we so richly deserve. And we do not need to associate pride with negativity. Now, would we all have the same admiration for its beauty if that peacock were to be all weary and frayed and did not strut about the way it did? I think not. Don't we all put on our best selves when we want to make an impression, especially to make ourselves attractive to someone else?

Me thinks the person who coined this simile must have been one envious person who did not stop to think!

So, what I am asking you to do here, is to STOP living on borrowed beliefs and perceptions. Learn to think for yourself, question your perceptions and beliefs, and then develop your perceptions to be in tune with who you are and what you believe.

CHAPTER 3

SELF AWARENESS

It is wisdom to know others.
it is enlightenment to know one's self.

Lao Tzu

WHAT IS SELF AWARENESS?

Self-awareness is not the narrative you tell yourself about yourself. It is about the reality of your actions and behaviour.

The capacity to observe your emotions and reactions is called self-awareness. It allows you to identify your strengths, weaknesses, what triggers and motivates you, and other characteristic traits. Being self-aware entails delving deeper into your emotions, why you feel the way you do, and how your feelings might manifest as reactions.

It is also the ability to look at your own actions and words from another's perspective, to view yourself as the world sees you. Is this more about objectivity than the way the world sees you? Trying to not have it clash with the idea of being authentic and not worrying about how someone else sees you.

Self-Awareness is the basis of authenticity. You can achieve authenticity only when you become aware of your core values and beliefs, your emotions, characteristics, and traits, and how they align with who you are and how you are perceived in the world.

"It is wisdom to know others; it is enlightenment to know one's self."
~ Lao-Tzu.

With this knowledge and insight, we can set goals for ourselves. We become aware of the capabilities that can help us grow further. Our strengths make us feel confident in our ability to improve our weaknesses.

When we are not self-aware, we tend to stay in a fixed mindset that does not allow us to change or move forward, leading us to stagnation or inertia and dissatisfaction with ourselves.

The more you learn to recognize your needs and desires and what you want in life, the closer you become to the real authentic version of yourself. The closer you stand in your light, the more powerful you become. And you attract the right people into your life.

The lyrics of the song "Man in the Mirror" by Michael Jackson best describe what self-awareness is to me.

How do I become self-aware?

The best way to learn to know yourself is to pay attention to your thoughts. The critical thoughts, the empathic thoughts you have for others. How you speak to or think about others, represents how you talk to or feel about yourself. Identify the harsh voice, the inner critic inside of you. In all likelihood, that is not your voice. That is an imbibed voice of a parent, teacher, or caregiver in your childhood. Silence the inner critic and harsh voice and find your inner voice.

Ask yourself what you are passionate about. What are the things you enjoy doing? What drives you? What brings you joy? What triggers you?
What makes you sad? What makes you mad?
Are you happy living the life you live, doing what you do? If not, what would you like to change?
What would you like to do more of in your life?
When was the last time you had fun? When was the last time you were carefree and childlike?

A child acts the way they want to without the fear of being judged. What are you able to do without the fear of being judged? What would you like to be doing if no one were judging you?
Identify them and incorporate them into your life.Identify beliefs that hold you back. Chances are they were not yours to begin with. Most of your beliefs have been passed down to you by parental or societal influence. Question your beliefs. Do they still serve you? Work with a coach, therapist, or counsellor if you need help managing independently.

Painful traumas or wounds may be too much to take on by yourself. Some might even find it hard to break old belief systems and patterns. While self-help books do help bring awareness of the possibility to change and overcome fears, some may need the guidance of a coach or counsellor.

How do I know if I am self-aware?

You are open to learning about yourself.

You are introspective. You look within.

You are open to feedback about yourself or your actions and take them positively.

You are not defensive or in denial about your weaknesses.

You identify your strengths and enhance them.

You question your beliefs, thoughts, and actions and determine what triggers them.

You acknowledge, identify and express your emotions freely.

You can acknowledge your mistakes and learn not to repeat them.

You admit to your mistakes and their impact on others and sincerely apologize.

You like to step out of your comfort zone and take chances.

You can make tough decisions.

You act on your goals and desires.

You focus on the present.

You have a vision of what you want the future to be.

What value does self-awareness add to my life?

Self-awareness gives you a better understanding of yourself and increases your self-esteem and confidence. It also helps you have more clarity, communicate better, and become a better decision-maker. It also enables you to understand and manage your emotions and empathize with others. Understand that self-awareness does not happen overnight. It is a life-long practice that requires commitment.

CHAPTER 4

BREAKING OLD PATTERNS & LIMITING SELF BELIEFS

The only limits that exist are the ones in your own mind.

Anonymous

WHAT IS A BELIEF SYSTEM?

A belief system is a set of beliefs and principles formed from experiences and inferences of incidents and situations. Belief systems are deeply ingrained subconsciously and are the navigation system that steers our direction in life. We tend to accept our beliefs as accurate even if they are not.

Your personal belief system significantly impacts your life and who you are, where you live, who you surround yourself with, what you think is acceptable or not, what is achievable or not, and how you live are all determined by your belief system.
Your belief system provides the foundation for your mental, emotional, physical, and spiritual well-being.

How are Belief Systems created?

Can you recall being carefree and spontaneous as a child? Children say what they want and act on their feelings without fearing what it sounds like to others. Psychologists believe that most of a child's belief system is formed by age seven. Children are like sponges and pick up everything taught to them and what they observe and experience. Parental influence as well as that of teachers and peers at school are formative in building a belief system in a child. Do you remember when you were a child, you were constantly taught to fit in, how to speak, and behave?

When we accept something as accurate and establish it as a belief, it gets stored in our subconscious mind. Our subconscious mind is unconcerned with whether a belief is true or incorrect. It merely saves it as a fact for future reference.

Our subconscious mind is our inbuilt navigation system to protect and keep us safe and secure. It aids in the automation of our behaviours and responses to specific situations.

E.g., If a child is consistently ignored by the parents every time they need attention, they can form a belief system that they are 'not good enough' or are 'unlovable'. And later, if the child is bullied or does poorly in school and is always put down or shouted at by the parents and teachers, those experiences will only reinforce the belief system that the child has already formed of not being good enough or being unlovable. These are limiting beliefs.

We continue to add to our belief system – both positive and limiting – through the various experiences we have in our lives.

What are Limiting Beliefs?

Some beliefs are positive and empowering, while others are negative and limiting. These limiting beliefs keep us from being our best selves, discovering our full potential, and achieving what we want. It also inhibits us from trying new experiences and being open to new opportunities. It can impact our self-worth and self-esteem, affecting our mental and emotional health.

Positive beliefs enable us to be resilient and believe in ourselves, generating positive thoughts and feelings.

"If you accept a limiting belief, then it will become a truth for you."

~

Louise Hay

Most people are unaware of their belief systems as they have yet to take the time to introspect and examine them. This is why some people are successful and prosper in the face of adversity while others fail. The good thing is that we can change our belief systems.

How can you change your Limiting Beliefs?

Identify your limiting beliefs.

Pay attention to your thoughts and what stories you tell yourself. Eg. I am not good enough. I am lazy. I am ugly. I am not creative. I am not successful. Write them down as they come to you. Journaling will help you see the patterns of thought and beliefs.

Evaluate and challenge them.

Examine each belief and see if it is true or if it is only your perception of it. Challenge the belief. As in, ask yourself where it came from. Whose voice do you remember telling you that you are lazy or not good enough? Question it further and delve deeper to see how it was formed and whether it is relevant to you today. Is it serving you now?

Overwrite it with a positive affirmation.

Reframe the negative into a positive sentence and affirm it to yourself every day.

Here are a few examples to help you.

Limiting belief:
I don't have the experience to do this job.
New empowering belief:
I am capable of taking on the challenge of this role.

Limiting belief:
I am lazy. I don't do enough.
New empowering belief:
I am active and productive and do as much as possible.

Limiting belief:
I am ugly.
New empowering belief:
I am beautiful just as I am.

Rewriting your limiting beliefs into positive ones is powerful and effective. **"Thoughts become things"**, so the way to do it is to believe in what you are saying. Now that you have held onto those old limiting beliefs for as long and as old as you are, remember it will not change overnight. Awareness is a step toward awakening, but action and repetitive action are necessary to overwrite the old beliefs. Say them to yourself every chance you get. While driving, as you wake up, before you go to bed. Write them on Post-its and stick them on your walls or your mirror. These will remind you to say them to yourself. It takes time and persistence; if you stay committed, you will get magical results. Old patterns start to break away, and you will feel lighter, motivated, and empowered to progress toward your dreams and goals.

Chapter 5

Dealing with Negative Emotions

I sat with my anger long enough

until she told me her real name was grief.

C. S. Lewis

THE GUEST HOUSE

This being human is a guest house.
Every morning a new arrival.
A joy, a depression, a meanness,
some momentary awareness comes
as an unexpected visitor.
Welcome and entertain them all!
Even if they're a crowd of sorrows,
who violently sweep your house
empty of its furniture,
still treat each guest honourably.
He may be clearing you out
for some new delight.
The dark thought, the shame, the malice,
meet them at the door laughing,
and invite them in.
Be grateful for whoever comes,
because each has been sent
as a guide from beyond.

~

Jalaluddin Rumi

WHAT ARE NEGATIVE EMOTIONS?
WHAT IS THE IMPACT OF HOLDING ON TO THEM?

Negative emotions include sadness, anger, fear, jealousy, anxiety, and hate. These are normal emotions that everyone feels during their lifetime. Negative emotions can make us dissatisfied with ourselves, others, and life. We also lose self-confidence and self-esteem when we allow them to impact our lives for extended periods. When our negative emotions control us, we have irrational thoughts and behaviours, losing perspective of what is true. This prevents us from genuinely enjoying life and dampens our enthusiasm to live wholly and completely.

SADNESS

Sadness is emotional pain that can arise from grief, loss, disappointment, deep distress, anguish, despair, or helplessness. It is a natural human emotion, and we experience it several times in our lifetime. Sadness weighs us down, while happiness uplifts us. Sadness is not a good feeling, but it is essential to feel it and acknowledge it rather than suppress it. While we are sad and weighted, we become slower in thought and movement. It allows us to slow down and reflect on the incidents that triggered it and may allow us to shift our mindset in understanding a situation. As a result, we pay attention to our emotional and mental health. We even get support from others when we are sad. It evokes compassion and empathy in others to help us. Deep, prolonged sadness, with other unresolved emotions, can lead to depression.

How to cope with sadness?

The first step would be to acknowledge that you are feeling sad and identify the triggers that made you feel sad. Don't try to deny that you are feeling low. Be okay with feeling sad. It is normal. It does not make you less if you acknowledge that you feel sad.

How to cope with Sadness?

Sit in silence, reflect on the situation and how it played out, and find what you need to learn from it and how to accept what is.

Avoid reaching out for unhealthy coping mechanisms like alcohol, drugs, binge eating, etc.

Reach out to friends and family for support.

Exercise is an excellent way to work out your sadness. Exercise releases feel-good hormones like dopamine and serotonin. Going for a jog, walk, or swim in nature will help you feel better.

Try to incorporate self-care. It is hard when you are feeling down, but the more you schedule some self-care into your routine, the better you will start to feel.

Know when it is time to seek professional help. If what you are doing has not been working for you and your sadness prolongs, it is better to seek help.

ANGER

Why do we feel Angry?

Anger is a normal healthy emotion that everyone experiences several times. We feel angry when boundaries are crossed, our expectations are unmet, or someone has done or said something that causes us pain. It is a natural emotional response to a perceived threat or unfairness. Anger ranges from mild irritation to annoyance, to wrath and full-blown rage. It evokes a reaction of one wanting to lash out or to be vengeful. Anger is the body's fight response to a threat, while sadness is a flight response. When sadness is repressed for an extended period, it can turn into anger.

While anger is controlled or reflected upon, it can lead to positive outcomes by determining what triggers your anger, recognising patterns, and where they come from. However, uncontrolled anger appears in aggressive behaviour, constant outbursts, retaliation, consistent road rage, and a negative outlook on the world.

What is Passive Aggression?

Passive-aggressive behaviour shows up when anger is often repressed and not expressed or acknowledged. The person shows it in various unhealthy and indirect forms, like passing snide remarks about a person who has angered you, agreeing with a person on a subject and later dissing the person and their views, being cynical towards a person.

{ I liken *'holding on to anger longer than needed to wearing sunglasses long after stepping out of the sun. Anger colours your world, and everything you see seems tainted. It even blocks the light that can come in.'* Light is a metaphor for kindness and healing. }

You can hold onto anger for so long that it becomes a part of who you are even though you may have long forgotten or repressed the incident that caused it. That changes your personality, your relationships, and your view of the world. Holding onto this unexpressed anger leads to depression, anxiety, being offensive, addictions to numb your feelings, self-harm, and harming others.

"I sat with my anger long enough until she told me her real name was grief."
~
C. S. Lewis.

How do we let go of anger?

Breathe. The first thing to do is consciously breathe and step back.

Acknowledge that you are angry. We often try to suppress our anger because, as children, it was conveyed that being angry is unacceptable. Once you acknowledge that you are angry, you can ask yourself why or what made you angry.

Review the incident that has caused you anger. Look at the situation objectively, not as a victim. Look at the patterns of the things that make you angry. Ask where it comes from. Revisit childhood experiences, and it often will go back to that.

Understand that everyone comes from a different place and carries their own baggage. Only hurt people give out hurt.

"No one can make you feel inferior without your consent."
Eleanor Roosevelt

Ask yourself what is the actual reason that caused you to experience anger. Were you slighted, put down, made to feel less than, ignored, unheard, disrespected, abused, or violated? Identify the feeling you got that precipitated the emotion of anger. Allow yourself to sit with it and feel it. It may cause you to cry, to be emotional. Allow, acknowledge, and then ask yourself what you learn from the incident. Your inner being will always let you know when you ask the right questions and learn from a situation. Every moment is a teaching moment, and sometimes the lessons are painful. And unless you learn from it, it will keep coming back bigger and bigger until you understand. Remember, pain is the most significant teacher!

Talk about it. Once you have processed your feelings and thoughts, and are in a calm space, talk about it to the person concerned or to someone you are close to or even journal about it.

Let it out in a healthy manner. If you cannot talk about it, I recommend to clients in therapy to write a letter to the person who upset them. You do not have to give the person the letter. Just write it, let the person know how their actions affected you, acknowledge all your feelings, and then burn or tear the letter up. This proves to be an excellent and effective technique to release and let go.

I can recall an incident in school. I was weak in Math. One day, I tried my best to get some geometry problems right, and the teacher turned around and said, "Someone must have done it for you." I was livid and upset because I had taken the trouble to get it right after many attempts. After that, I developed an aversion to the subject because of my anger towards the teacher. I just gave up trying. And the more I ignored and dodged it, the poorer my grades got. Finally, it was apparent to my parents that I needed help, and they got me a fabulous, patient, and kind tutor, and he helped me understand the subject and take a liking to it. His help restored my confidence in myself and my capabilities. The key was getting help; the same goes for our emotional pain. It is okay to get help, to talk it out with the person calmly, or to talk to someone about it. In cases of trauma, rape, abuse, or consistent toxic environments, it is advisable to seek the help of a counsellor.

You only have the present moment, so don't let the past dictate your present and ruin your future. Take charge and liberate yourself from the power anger has over-you.

FEAR

Fear is a protective, instinctual emotion that we experience. It protects us from harm or impending danger. Fears are developed or learned based on our past experiences, society, and the culture surrounding us.

The two primal fears that we are born with are ~ Fear of heights and fear of loud noises.

Having a healthy dose of fear is essential to survival, as it cautions a person to stay safe. However, we often build up fears for various situations that are not potentially harmful in the scenario but are to our well-being and keep us from being authentic and discovering our potential.

E.g., fear of public speaking, fear of the dark, fear of staying alone, fear of traveling alone.

Rational fear is when there is a clear and present danger. **Irrational fears** and phobias are extreme unwarranted fears linked to a specific object or event. These are the fears that keep us from living our best lives. Some of these are — Fear of what people think, fear of the unknown, fear of change, fear of failure, fear of success.

To understand the difference between rational and irrational fears is to overcome our fears. Identify your fears and see where they come from. Most often, parents and society succeed in transferring fears to others and their children. The media plays a massive role in creating fears through pessimistic reporting.

"The fears we don't face become our limits"

Robin Sharma

Past experiences are also a foundation- Being bitten by a dog or having unhealthy relationships. The truth is, not every dog will be ferocious, and not every relationship will be terrible. However, we stay stuck in the trauma of the situation and find it hard to let go and move on; this is how we stay stuck in our fears.

{ To me: *'Fear is a lack of faith and belief in one's capabilities and the lack of faith in a Higher Power to protect and guide us.'* }

What is the benefit of facing and overcoming fears?

The payoff in overcoming a fear is the liberation to grow and live freely. The feeling of freedom and accomplishment, and the victory you feel is incomparable. An example here is of me being a writer. As a kid in school, I got such negative remarks for any written assignment I submitted. Most of the comments were that I was untidy. The experience was so humiliating that I eventually gave up writing. I went through most of college, only submitting assignments if I had to. Much later, writing came to me much more easily as I overcame the fear of being judged and not being good enough. I soon discovered I wanted to be a writer and share my knowledge and experiences in life! So here I am writing, unsure if I am good at it or if it will appeal to many or a few, but just writing because I like to share my transformative experiences in the hope that it might help someone to overcome their fears and become who they want to be. I did start smaller, writing speeches and blogs, and have finally begun authoring a book.

'Everything you desire is on the other side of fear."

~

Bob Proctor

How can we overcome our fears?

In coaching, I often ask my clients: "What's the worst that can happen?" I tell them to question all the answers they come up with and challenge the assumptions until they drill down to the answer, they're at peace with.

Acknowledge your fears.

Ask yourself what you are fearful about. Weigh different outcomes if you were to do something. Then you will be able to identify your real fears.

List all your fears.

Then start with a couple where you feel least fearful. Address the one where you are least afraid. And then move to the next. This will help you build confidence in yourself.

Plan on how you intend to face a fear.

Form affirmations in your mind or write them down repeatedly. Eg. I make amazing cakes. I am a fabulous baker. (If you have a fear of baking).

Look at your excuses.

Call yourself out on them. Eg. For the last few years, I would make up excuses to start drafting this book, saying I was too busy or tired. I have a fear of not being perfect. And until I convinced myself that there is no such thing as perfection, I was able to start writing this book.

Don't look for perfection. Start small. We are all perfect in our imperfections. You can fall a few times but pick yourself up and start again. Make small goals at first before you target bigger goals.

Surround yourself with confident and successful people.

Just as decay spreads, so do confidence and self-esteem. If you surround yourself with people who overcome their fears and achieve something, you can learn from them.

Do not worry about failing.
No one has ever achieved success without failing a few times. "Failures are the stepping stones to success."

And lastly, you need to **let go of the fear of what others think or say about you.** When you do have that fear, you relinquish all your power to them and will never be able to overcome any of your fears or achieve any of your goals.

Many years ago, I used to play Candy Crush to unwind. It is one of the most popular and iconic match-three puzzle games Picture a grid filled with colourful candies of various shapes and sizes. The player has to swap adjacent candies to create rows or columns of three or more matching candies. The game keeps things interesting with various levels, each with its own unique challenges. You might need to collect a certain number of candies, clear jellies, or reach a specific score—all within a limited number of moves. Oh, and the special candies! Make a match of four or more, and you get these powerful treats that can wipe out rows, columns, or even whole sections of the board. It's a sweet symphony of strategy and luck, all wrapped up in a candy-coated package. Ever given it a go?

While playing the game, I observed that I had never seen the word 'failed' so many times at anything but in this game, and yet I went back and replayed those levels every time without ever giving up. And I asked myself if this were a real-life situation, would I have given up or relentlessly pursued my goals to succeed? That is when I realized that only our fear of judgement and others' opinions keep us from pursuing our goals and dreams. This certainly gave me a lot of insight into my fears and helped me overcome my fear of the 'court of public opinion.'

I recently watched an animated movie called **'Spirit Untamed.'** On seeing me watch an animated film, my son was like, "What are you doing watching an animated movie? You're not a kid." *(An example of a stereotyped/ belief system right there).* Anyway, I watched it through to the end, enjoyed it, and heard the most fantastic song, which turned out to be perfect to share here. I now know I was meant to watch the movie to share the song with you. **"Fearless" by Isabella Merced.**

Please listen to the song on You Tube or Spotify to experience it.

JEALOUSY AND ENVY

Jealousy and Envy are both a result of the feeling of being inadequate.

Envy is the feeling of coveting what someone else has, a talent, a possession, a skill, or an attribute. Envy may not warrant any ill feelings towards the person with what you want. Comparison is the root of envy.

Jealousy is more personal of the two. It arises from feelings of insecurity, fear of losing something or someone, or the threat of being replaced.

With jealousy, fear is involved. Feelings of anger, resentment, insecurity, and hostility often accompany it. Depending on the severity of the emotion, it can lead to irrational thoughts, behaviours, and mistrust.

How do I deal with Jealousy?

Be honest with how you feel. If you feel threatened in a relationship, be open and acknowledge it. Communicate it to your partner.

Identify your insecurities. Ask yourself where you feel inferior and why you do so.

Acknowledge your abilities. If you are jealous that someone makes more money than you, look for areas where you can make changes in your life to earn more money and how you can achieve that with your skills and capabilities. Learn to value who you already are.

Make gratitude a practice. Be grateful for what you already have. Acknowledge and recognise all that is going well for you.

Evaluate your expectations. Be mindful of your expectations. Are they realistic or not?

Stop comparing yourself to others. Find a more balanced resolution to your issues.

ANXIETY

Anxiety arises from the fear of the unknown or the inability to predict how a situation or event may pan out. It is a worry about the future. Anxiety is a normal reaction in stressful situations. It can also be beneficial, like being more alert in dangerous situations.

Anxiety comes with the feeling of fear, nervousness, dread, uneasiness, tension, and overthinking. When these feelings persist and start interfering with daily life, it could become an anxiety disorder. Panic attacks stem from anxiety.

How do I deal with Anxiety?

Deep breathing exercises help reduce anxiety.

Identify the triggers and break them down. Observe your thought patterns. Challenge your negative thoughts to see if they are true or just perceptions.

Establish a good sleep schedule.

Journal before going to bed.

Meditation helps ease anxiety.

Exercise helps release restless energy. It also increases feel-good hormones in the body.

Flip negative thoughts into positive ones. Eg. I am not good at public speaking, to - I can speak well and confidently on a stage.

Talk to someone about your anxiety. If it interferes with your daily habits, seek professional help.

GUILT

Guilt is an emotion based on morality. When you feel that you have compromised your ethics and codes of conduct which are either personal or universal in nature, you feel guilt. When you believe you have upset or offended someone and feel responsible, you feel guilt. When you make a mistake and may have done or said things in anger and that do not resonate with you normally, you may feel regret and guilt.

I have encountered a lot of people who have regrets when they haven't picked up a call from a friend or loved one, or not replied to a text, or even had an argument and then they hear that the person passed on. This causes a lot of regret and guilt. There is no way for anyone to know they might not have another chance. The guilt will only weigh you down further and for sure the person who passed on isn't going to be holding a grudge that you didn't call or text them back.

How do I overcome Guilt?

Acknowledge that you are feeling guilty.

Delve deeper into the specifics of the incident that you feel guilty from.

If it involves upsetting or hurting someone, take steps to apologise or resolve misunderstandings that you might have caused.

Accept that you are not perfect and that everyone makes mistakes.

Learn from the mistakes and move on.

Remember who you are otherwise and lift yourself up to know that you are not your mistakes.

Remember that in that moment you made a choice, which may not have been the best and learn from it and how you can do better the next time.

Stop focusing on the incident and letting it consume you.

Show compassion to yourself.

Put someone else in your position and see if you can observe it objectively.

Have clear boundaries on what you can or cannot do. Sometimes unclear boundaries, being stretched in too many directions can leave you frayed and cause you to make choices which do not benefit you.

Express your remorse to the person concerned.

Take responsibility for your actions.

Forgive yourself.

Move on with all that you have learnt.

SHAME

Shame is an uncomfortable feeling you experience of inadequacy and unworthiness.

When your vulnerabilities are exposed and open to judgement, you also feel shame. We all experience this unpleasant emotion when we are embarrassed by our thoughts and actions which are considered improper.

While guilt is the feeling of 'doing' something wrong, shame is the feeling of 'being' wrong, bad, or inferior. It is more personal than guilt.

While guilt in a way is productive as it helps to redirect us into making better choices, shame often leads people into self-destructive behaviours.

Shame is rooted in fear. When we are humiliated, rejected, tormented, or abused, we feel shame. Shame is also the root cause of anger.

"Where perfectionism exists,
shame is always lurking."
Brene Brown

As Brene Brown explains it, "It's not what I do that isn't good enough. It's the who I am that is unacceptable."

Your conscious mind tells you, you can do better, it's your subconscious mind that stops you from doing it, to protect you from feeling ashamed that you will not be good enough.

How do I overcome feelings of Shame?

Recognise and acknowledge that you have shame.

Show kindness and compassion to yourself.

Show empathy to yourself.

Know that no one is perfect, and that includes all the people you think are perfect.
Practice self-love.

Separate yourself from the negative voices that belittle you.

Understand that your failures are not you! They are actions that can be learnt from and changed.

Establish clear boundaries.

Break free from toxic relationships.

If you have deep toxic shame which results in substance abuse, toxic relationships, social anxiety, or low self-esteem, please seek professional help.

CHAPTER 6

FORGIVENESS & LETTING GO

True forgiveness is being able to say thank you for that experience.

Oprah Winfrey

FORGIVENESS

Forgiveness is the conscious decision to let go and move on from an experience or person that has caused you pain, anger, or sadness. "Forgiveness is the act of pardoning an offender. In the Bible, the Greek word translated as "forgiveness" literally means "to let go," as when a person does not demand payment for a debt." The same is true for forgiving yourself.

As a kid, I recall when we fought, parents, teachers, or any adult told us to shake hands, say sorry to one another, and end the matter there. They did not encourage us to talk about our feelings or learn how our actions impacted another. In all probability, we kept repeating the behaviour. As adults, we are often able to analyse how our actions affect others or the impact their actions have on us. It is a choice to either stay wounded or to forgive and move on. And it does not come easy.

What Forgiveness does not mean

Condoning the other person's actions or saying what they did was okay:
Making excuses for a bully or bad behaviour is not forgiveness.

Sweeping it under the carpet or acting like it never happened.
Forgiveness does not mean being a doormat and allowing others to mistreat you. Being in denial of the abuse you go through is only you not standing up for yourself. When you allow others to take advantage of you, it simply shows them that the more you accept, the more they can use you. If you accept crap, you will get heaps of it. If you have boundaries and take what is worthy of you, you will get the respect you deserve.

Being besties with the person again:

When we have had hurtful experiences with someone, it does not mean we have to return to what once was. We all change and evolve, and sometimes certain occasions warrant keeping our distance from people who inflict pain on us repeatedly or cause us profound harm.

"Forgiveness is not about forgetting, it is remembering without pain."

We can see an incident as a one-off situation where the person had stressors that caused them to behave in a particular manner or if the incident repeats itself often enough to see it as a pattern with no learning and change. And we are responsible for the action we take. Our ego gets more bruised or offended than our soul in most situations. For the soul looks with compassion. Forgiveness is about letting go of the pain, healing the wounds, and moving forward to stand up to a more whole and complete you.

By looking into a situation where we are wounded, we can also allow ourselves to see objectively the part we have played.

When we let go of emotions and experiences that do not serve us, we reclaim our power to be ourselves. We disallow the person or incident to dominate our thoughts and actions. We do not have to go out and be BFFs once again. It only means that their actions have no control over you. And letting go does not mean suppressing your feelings. That's like putting a band-aid on a wound that needs deeper care. If we ignore it, it will fester into something more toxic. And as for anything to heal, we need to heal from within. That comes from knowing what actions/words hurt us and why. It often leads to more profound healing.

What are the effects of holding onto anger and past wounds without letting go?

We stay consumed with anger, and it clouds our perspective. We carry it along into every situation and relationship.

We become so consumed with being the victim that we feel helpless.

We stay stuck in the past and cannot enjoy the present.

We carry a weight with us that can lead to depression and anxiety.

We miss out on great opportunities and relationships because we stay stuck in the pain of past wounds.

We lose hope and can't see the joy in anything.

We want to bring everyone down around us to match our feelings and vibrations.

"Forgive people in your life, even those who are not sorry for their actions or even deny them. Holding onto anger only hurts you, not them."

How do we forgive?

Forgiveness takes time. It takes time to process your emotions and the experience and release what does not serve you. It all depends on the individual.

The first thing is to acknowledge your pain. Please don't deny it. The question to ask yourself is, how did this incident hurt me? What may have caused the incident? What is the learning for me in this situation?

The next step is to remove yourself from the said incident and try to look at it objectively. It might also help to write about it and how it impacted you or journal about it. You can even talk about it with someone who is an active listener. It will allow you to process the incident and your feelings.

I suggest that my clients write a letter to the person, expressing how they hurt them and how it impacted them. You do not have to give this letter to the person. It will help you process your emotions and release them. Burn or tear up the letter. It will make you feel much better.

When you are calmer and may have to address the situation with the person, you should talk about it one-on-one with the person concerned. Express your feelings calmly and honestly. Listen to what the other person has to say objectively.

Try to be empathic and show compassion to the person. This might seem difficult to comprehend when you are upset. But put yourself in the other person's shoes. Do not make excuses for them but ask yourself what you would have done in that position. You may sometimes get the answer you are looking for. It could give you an insight into who the person is and may help you reach a stage of acceptance and make you realise you cannot change what has happened, but you have a choice of staying stuck in it or letting it go and continuing with your life.

How do I know I have not let go or forgiven?

If it still consumes you and occupies your mind, you know you haven't let go. If you still have raw emotions about it, you have not let it go. If it is repetitive behaviour, you would probably need to look at your boundaries and how much you have been putting up with them. In everything, there is learning. Through these incidents, we learn about ourselves as well.

The past can define you only if you allow it to. Try to bring yourself into the present moment and ask yourself what choices you can make right now that are healthy for you.

Forgiving someone who has no remorse or has never admitted or acknowledged the pain they have caused you. Now this is one of the toughest situations that one can encounter and I am sure we all have at some point. What I have realised is, the person's fear of looking within and acknowledging their missteps, prevent them from admitting to the deed, because then they will have to acknowledge all their misdeeds and own up to them. That would be too daunting for someone who is not self-aware. So they would rather convince themselves that they did not do anything wrong. And if you have had this experience, it can be tough to forgive someone who shows no remorse. But it is in letting go that you free yourself from the pain and anger that you endured so that you do not continue to suffer. The person who hurt you remains oblivious and unaffected, and this may anger you further. Here is where I believe that you do what you have to do to let go and forgive and live in peace and let karma take care of the rest. It is from such experiences, that we learn to set better boundaries, become aware of our instincts and intuition and be true to yourself, so that you do not allow it to become a repetitive pattern.

What can I do to move forward?

We forgive by letting go of vengeful thoughts and wanting to get back at the person. We can rest well in knowing that God, the Universe, or karma will take care of it.

Forgiveness is a choice. A choice that benefits you more than the offender. By forgiving a person, you are releasing their control over you.

You know when you have forgiven someone when you wish them no ill will, when you can pray for them to find their light. And when you remember them or the incident, it no longer causes you pain or anger. There is no charge left for it. You can accept that it happened, and it did cause you grief when it did, and now you have moved on.

There are incidents where we feel guilty about our actions, requiring us to forgive ourselves too. To acknowledge, own, and learn from our mistakes is imperative. Making better choices and not repeating and offending others again makes it easier to forgive ourselves and move forward.

"You will only begin to heal when you let go of past hurts,
forgive those who have wronged you,
and learn to forgive yourself for your mistakes."

One of the most powerful, magical practices of forgiveness is The Ho'oponopono Prayer, which is a Hawaiian practise of forgiveness and reconciliation. In English it roughly translates to, "to make it right!" or to "bring things into balance" In this prayer one acknowledges that on some level we have played a part and are responsible for our own emotions and experiences.
It is made up of four simple sentences that you can chant several times with the person or situation in mind.

{ "I am sorry. Please forgive me. Thank you. I love you." }

With "I am sorry" you acknowledge that you may have played a part in the situation, knowingly or unknowingly, even by means of accepting certain behaviours.
"Please forgive me" evokes forgiveness not only with others but for yourself and for what you put up with.
"Thank you" is expressing gratitude in acknowledging the lessons learned, both positive and negative, because it these experiences that teach us to grow and evolve.
"I love you" is invoking the unconditional Universal love that is the most powerful source of healing to you and to all parties concerned.

I have found this to be most magical and miraculous. I use it to diffuse any tense situation, or even before I approach someone who is angry and wound up and it immediately calms the situation. It is one of the best tools for forgiveness, that immediately lightens you up, because you actually acknowledge that a there has been hurt or wrongful action that has occurred.

FORGIVENESS

How does Forgiving benefit us?

It makes you feel free and lighter, which in turn
helps you focus on the things that are important for your well-being.

It enables you to have better relationships.

To be more productive as a person.

You are happier when the anger and pain are released.

Your physical and psychological health improves.

You view everything more positively.

You regain control of your emotions and well-being by not letting others' actions control you.

You find compassion and understanding.

"Forgiveness
is the most powerful thing you can do for yourself.
If you can't learn to forgive,
you can forget about achieving true success in your life."

~

Wayne Dyer

Forgiving One's Self

Many times, we may have offended someone either consciously or unconsciously. We first need to take responsibility for our words or actions that have caused someone pain and suffering.

We may feel ashamed of our actions and hold resentment for ourselves for a long time. Or we may also deny how our actions have affected someone. Listen to what they tell you about how your actions impacted them.

It is as important to forgive ourselves, just as we forgive others.

If you seek forgiveness from the offended person, follow the same process.

Ask yourself what made you do or say what you did.

How did it affect the other person?

What can you change in yourself so as not to repeat offensive behaviour?

What can you do to earn the other person's forgiveness?

Process it before you meaningfully apologise.

Be honest and genuine in your apology. Ask how you can make it better.

Show remorse for what you have said or done. Make changes to back up your remorse. Your words and corresponding actions need to match for someone to believe you. Making empty promises will not get you anywhere.
Letting go of the shame and guilt will be easier when you start making changes in a positive direction. Your self-worth will improve, and you can build trust and confidence in having healthy relationships again.

Forgive and love yourself. Please acknowledge that you made a mistake and you learned from it. **You are not your mistake**

Chapter 7

Personal Boundaries & Prioritizing Oneself

Seek out those

who Inspire and Support You

Personal Boundaries

What are Personal Boundaries?

Personal Boundaries are unseen guidelines and limits you set for yourself of what behaviours are and are not acceptable to you. Setting boundaries helps you establish respectful, reciprocal, and mutually appropriate relationships. They are a way of protecting our energy, time, and space. Physical boundaries outline your need for physical space, touch, your eating, and sleeping habits etc. Emotional boundaries are indicative of your feelings and if you are comfortable sharing them.

What is the importance of having healthy boundaries?

Setting healthy personal boundaries, gives you a clearer perspective of who you are, what works for you and what doesn't in alignment with your beliefs and values. It also helps you develop a sense of identity and improves self-esteem. Establishing healthy boundaries allows you to express your thoughts and feelings in a way that communicates your needs effectively to others.

Healthy boundaries are essential for self-love. Without boundaries, you feel exhausted, exploited, taken for granted, or used. Poor boundaries, in your professional as well as personal lives can lead to resentment, hurt, rage, and burnout.

You know you do not have healthy boundaries when:

You are a PEOPLE PLEASER.

We often lose ourselves in our endeavour to please others, often to the point that we don't know who we are anymore. We end up floating through life running with the advice and suggestion of others. Many of us become conscious of our people pleasing habits, but do not know how to change it. To allow yourself to change you need to become aware of a few things.

Identify your need or reason to be liked by others or to please others all of the time. Where does your insecurity lie? What are the reasons you do this? Is it learned behaviour that has been passed down or simply because you have insecurities or fears of being rejected.

You WANT TO BE LIKED BY EVERYONE and care what others think of you.

Understand that it is okay not to be liked by everyone. In a world of a billion people, not everyone can always be liked. As goes with you too, you may only like some people you meet and know. No two individuals are alike, whether in a friendship, relationship, or even the family you are born into. There are things we love about those close to us and things we don't. In close relationships, the traits, or commonalities we resonate with, often outweigh the ones that don't, and this is what makes the relationship work. We choose to focus on the characteristics we love instead of the ones we don't. Unless it is too glaring an issue that cannot be ignored, it is okay not to be liked by everyone.

You are UNABLE TO SAY NO and let yourself be taken advantage of.

Saying yes to doing something for someone should be a matter of choice and not an obligation. You do not need to offer explanations and justifications to anyone. If something is not okay with you, it simply is not okay. You need not do or act on someone else's behalf if it does not align with your beliefs and values.

"NO! is a complete sentence"

you might have often heard. Use it. Learning to say no, is freeing, and liberating. Initially it is tough, but it gets easier the more one uses it.

Ask yourself why others will not take a no from you, but can say no to you in a heartbeat? Do you feel like you are being used or taken advantage of in certain relationships? A relationship is about give and take. Recognise the equations in your relationships and ask yourself if you are happy if the equation is not equal. If you are unhappy, ask yourself what you would like to change and how you can do it. Learn to value yourself more than to care about what they think of you.

You are constantly INVOLVED IN OTHER PEOPLE'S DRAMA and consider yourself the mediator or saviour.

This comes from a need of avoidance. When we do not want to focus on our own lives and improve our own situations, we find it easier to give our attention to other people's problems. We do that to feel good about ourselves, that we have helped someone. We can also get involved deeply to feel wanted and valued by someone. What tends to happen is that the more we start being available to others' dramas, the more pulled in we get and the more repetitive it gets.

The way to get out of it is to consciously take a step back and ask yourself how it is serving you? Think of the other things you can be doing for yourself instead? Be objective of the situation and think logically before getting your emotions involved. Having empathy and sympathy are two different things. When you show sympathy, you pity the person and downplay their capabilities to get themselves out of their own situation. You allow them to play the victim, instead of empowering them to take charge of their own lives.

To quote Michelle Obama here:

"Walk away from friendships that
make you feel small & insecure and
seek out people who inspire and support you."

How do we build Healthy Boundaries?

Take the time to know what works for you and what doesn't.

Be assertive. Learn to say NO!

Be honest and straightforward in communicating what you want to.

Do not overshare details of your life with people you may not know or trust.

CHAPTER 8

PRACTICING SELF LOVE

Love yourself first,
and everything else falls into line.

Lucille Ball

SELF LOVE

Self-Love is the acceptance of oneself wholly and completely without judgement. It means that you are aware that you are perfect in all your imperfections. Self-Love also means treating yourself with kindness and respect and nurturing your well-being, growth, and evolution.

Self-Love does not mean being narcissistic and self-absorbed. It is about showing compassion to ourselves. Just as we award kindness and compassion to others, it is about appreciating yourself for all that you are and honouring your needs.

Self-Love is doing the things that need to be done that help you evolve, grow, and shine your light in the world. It is a love that enables you to lead a better, happier life and be more in tune with who you were born to be, your authentic self. It isn't about your wants but your need to improve and work on your goals and purpose.

What does self-love look or feel like?

Being kinder to yourself and speaking kindly to yourself.

Appreciating yourself for who you are and all that you do.

Laying down boundaries of what is acceptable to you.

Not allowing yourself to be taken advantage of.

Being assertive.

Recognising and fulfilling your needs.

Forgiving yourself for when you fall short.

Playing to your strengths.

Letting go of negative emotions that hold you back.

Prioritising things that enhance your wellness.

Following your passions and doing things that bring you joy.

Finding your tribe. People who support and elevate you.

Valuing yourself, your presence, your identity and all that you are.

What is the importance of Self-Love?

The first step to practising Self-Love is to remember that we are not perfect. As humans, we make mistakes and that it is okay to make them. "It's okay to be not okay." Self-Love entails having respect for yourself and honouring your needs, mind, body, and soul. It encourages us to form healthy habits and makes us motivated to be better and do better.

Self-Love enables you to have healthier boundaries, better relationships, more self-esteem, being whole and complete in yourself. You are then able to identify your values, your goals and purpose. It also helps you be calm in the face of adversity by acknowledging your capabilities, believing in yourself and being at peace with who you are.

Recognize your worth: Appreciate yourself for all that you are. Recognize your talents, capabilities, and strengths. Be grateful for them. Nurture yourself, your health, and your skills. Even if you have any mental, physical, or weight issues, learn to love yourself, for it is that body that carries you through the day and enables you to do all you do daily. Give thanks for it. It is only when you learn to appreciate yourself, that you start caring for yourself. Take time for self-care. That could be exercising, eating healthy, taking a spa day, spending time on things you love to do, whether it is reading a book, dancing, singing, painting, or whatever else. Look after your mind, body, and spirit. It is you and only you that can know what you need and do it for yourself.

The more you learn to recognize your needs and desires and what you want in life, the closer you get to be the real authentic version of yourself. The closer you get to stand in your light, the more powerful you become.

" How you love yourself is how you teach others to love you."

~

Rupi Kaur

SELF LOVE

Steps to Achieving Self-Love:

Don't compare yourself to others.

Don't let others' opinions of you dictate who you are.

Don't fear failure. Failures or mistakes are the stepping stones to success.

Learn to step away from toxic situations and toxic relationships.

Spend time with people who value you and elevate you.

Face your fears, don't hide from them.

Believe in yourself and the power you have within you.

Prioritize yourself and your needs.

Allow yourself to acknowledge and feel all your emotions.

Acknowledge your wins and appreciate yourself for them.

Step out of your comfort zone.
Start with small tasks and build your confidence.

SELF LOVE

Stay focused on your goals.
Change how you approach them but never lose sight of them.

Form healthy habits that enhance your well-being.

You are a soul, don't let your physical appearance define who you are.

Be unafraid to speak your truth.

You are enough.
You don't have to strive to be more to be more worthy than you are already are.

Find the beauty and joy in nature, gestures, kindness, and generosity.

Live in gratitude.

Spend time alone with yourself.

Do things that nourish your soul.
Get creative and work with your hands.

Sit in silence. Meditate. Contemplate. Journal.

Be uniquely you!
Love and appreciate yourself wholly and entirely,
for you are one of a kind. There isn't another you.

"GIVE
YOURSELF
TIME

TO PAUSE

AND
JUST
BREATHE"

BREATHE

She sat at the back, and they said she was shy,
She led from the front, and they hated her pride,
They asked her advice and then questioned her guidance,
They branded her loud, then were shocked by her silence,
When she shared no ambition, they said it was sad,
So she told them about her dreams, and they said she was mad,
They told her they'd listen, then covered their ears,
And gave her a hug while they laughed at her fears,
And she listened to all of it, thinking she should,
Be the girl they told her to be best as she could,
But one day, she asked what was best for herself,
Instead of trying to please everyone else,
So she walked to the forest and stood with the trees,
She heard the wind whisper and dance with the leaves,
She spoke to the willow, the elm, and the pine,
And she told them what she'd been told time after time,
She told them she felt she was never enough,
She was either too little or far, too much,
Too loud or too quiet, too fierce or too weak,
Too wise or too foolish, too bold or too meek,
Then she found a small clearing surrounded by firs,
And she stopped...and she heard what the trees said to her,
And she sat there for hours, not wanting to leave,
For the forest said nothing, it just let her breathe.

by Becky Helmsley

CHAPTER 9

MEDITATION

The goal of meditation
is not to control your thoughts,
but to stop letting them control you.

MEDITATION

What is Meditation?

Meditation refers to various practices that focus on aligning the mind, body, and soul. Meditation is training your mind in focus and awareness. It also means to sit in silence and observe, be non-judgemental, and be mindful of the present moment. Breathwork aids you in getting into a relaxed meditative state.

Meditation does not require you to suppress your thoughts and emotions. It allows you to quiet the voices in your mind of worry, anxiety, fear, and other negative emotions by observing them instead of engaging with them. By not judging yourself or your thoughts, it means to just observe them without putting any positive or negative charge to it, or taking a moral standing and deeming it right or wrong. It is about simply observing and going 'Hmmm, interesting" and let it be and not engage with the though t.

Meditation is training the mind just as physical exercise is for the body.

There are several types of meditation. Some involve focussing on a particular sensation, such as breathing, sounds, visualisation, or on an object like a candle flame or chanting a mantra.

Meditation has been a part of Indian history for thousands of years, and many meditative techniques began in various Asian countries as well.

The Monkey Mind, a term coined by The Buddha, describes the part of the brain responsible for all the mind chatter, flits from one thing to another, and is easily distracted. It is a loud voice in our minds that is fear-based and insists on being heard. It is the part of the brain that connects with the inner critic and the ego. The monkey mind most often debilitates our movement forward to pursue our passions and stifles our creativity. And that is how The Buddha learned to meditate to silence the monkey mind and taught his disciples to tame the monkeys in their minds and take control.

So the 3 parts that meditation involves:

Observing your thoughts.

Being non judgmental

Quietening the Monkey Mind

{ I find this video on You Tube explains the Monkey Mind well.
https://www.youtube.com/watch?v=t-JiQubfMPg&ab_channel=YongeyMingyurRinpoche
https://www.youtube.com/watch?v=qxyVCjp48S4&ab_channel=Headspace }

Getting Started

Meditation is not easy initially, just like anything you learn for the first time. It takes a lot of practice. It is like exercising, painful to begin, and it starts to feel better when we consistently put in the work. I do not mean physically painful. You can get distracted easily. Your thoughts wander, you get a bit frustrated, and you develop self-doubt about your meditating ability. But if you persist, you will get there and enjoy and benefit from it. What it requires is for you to sit in silence, and you can start with just 5 minutes each time you would like to meditate. You can do it twice a day, once when you wake up, before you start your day and once at the end of the day, before you sleep.

It took me almost a year to learn to meditate. At first, my thoughts would wander, I couldn't sit still, and I would be restless. I started with breathwork and listening to guided meditations. I used to be an insomniac and had trouble sleeping. So, I listened to guided meditations to help me fall asleep. Initially, it would take about three guided meditations to calm my mind. I did, however, train my mind in the process to listen. After gaining confidence in meditating, I went to Dharamshala in Northern India. I did a Buddhist Meditation course there to advance my learning. Since then, I have meditated regularly, developed a great sense of clarity and calmness, and feel more aligned with myself.

What are the benefits of Meditation?

Reduces stress and anxiety

Improves focus and mental alertness

Brings a sense of calmness and peace

Helps you feel grounded and centred

Opens the door to spiritual growth by connecting you to your inner voice.

Increases Self Awareness

Enhances physical and mental wellness when you learn to focus on the present moment without judgement.

Brings clarity in thought and decision making.

Helps transform fears

What are the several types of Meditation?

Transcendental meditation is a simple, natural technique where you silently repeat a word, sound, or phrase known as a mantra. The mantras come from the ancient Vedic texts of India and are Sanskrit sounds. Om' is considered the original vibration of the universe. And so chanting it is a way of literally resonating with all existence. If you are more comfortable with words or phrases that resonate and have more meaning to you, you can always chant another word. Eg. Peace, Calm, I can and I will, Life is good!

Mindfulness meditation is another form of meditation that is extremely popular. It requires you to observe your thoughts and feelings without judging or engaging with them.

Guided meditation. These are meditations led by a teacher or an audio recording of a voice that leads you through guided imagery or visualization. In this method of meditation, you form mental pictures of scenery or a situation that relaxes you. You may be instructed to use one or more senses, such as sights, smells, sounds, and touch.

Mantra meditation. In this type of meditation, you chant a calming word, thought, or affirmation to keep focus.

There is also **Walking meditation**, where one walks slower and is conscious of every step and sensation when walking. One can meditate while communing with nature.

Eating meditation is another way to be mindful of all the thoughts and sensory experiences one has while eating every morsel of a meal. It means being completely present and observant of every experience detail.

Focused exercises that enable you to meditate are Yoga, Tai chi, and Qi gong. These exercises allow you to restore balance through physical movement, focus, and relaxation.

How to Practice Meditation on your own?

The basics of meditation are setting a time every day to form a routine. Early mornings work well, or any time you are free. Set a timer for 10 minutes initially. Make sure you are seated in a comfortable position with your spine erect. Wear loose, comfortable clothing.

Counting: 4-2-4 Method.

You can start by simply breathing. Inhale for four counts, hold for two and exhale for four counts. The counts keep your monkey mind focused on counting the numbers and help you to calm your mind significantly.

You can also do a 4-7-8 Method.

Inhale for 4, hold for seven, and exhale for eight counts.

These are good calming meditations, to begin with. As you progress, you can explore guided meditations. A vast choice is available on the internet and YouTube.

The counting method is most effective for a beginner, as it helps to occupy the mind by counting, keeping it from wandering.

Here are some videos to help you start:

https://www.youtube.com/watch?v=4qACPNA2cKY&ab_channel=Hands-OnMeditation

https://www.youtube.com/watch?v=7WnZisfYMsE&ab_channel=MasterClass

https://www.youtube.com/watch?v=ssss7V1_eyA&ab_channel=GreatMeditation

https://www.youtube.com/watch?v=zyUy9w953L0&ab_channel=GreatMeditation

You can also find meditation in various creative activities like painting, listening to music, dancing, writing, and crafting. If you're fully immersed, being "in the zone" without letting your mind wander, staying completely engrossed and immersed in the activity of participation, that would also be a meditation. Your entire focus and concentration are on the activity you are engaged in. E.g., An athlete before a race or an actor in character playing a part.

Chapter 10

What is Journaling

Journal writing is a voyage to the interior

-

Christina Baldwin

JOURNALING

How is Journaling beneficial?

Thoughts constantly occupy our minds. When we have issues, our thoughts revolve around those issues, and we continuously dwell on the subject. It feels like our thoughts are constantly playing on the loop until we find a solution to the problem we face. We release these thoughts when we share a problem with another person. However, sometimes, we may not want to share the problem as it may be too personal. This is where journaling is beneficial. When we pour our thoughts and feelings onto paper which is a very non-judgemental space, it helps release the thoughts from our mind. This process allows us to free up our minds, clarify, and establish recurring thought patterns. We can enable solution-oriented ideas to enter rather than stay stuck on the problem.

Journaling also helps us get to know more about ourselves. When we write down our thoughts and feelings about our experiences, we can observe our thought patterns and what causes us to feel a certain way or react to certain things. Who or what triggers specific emotions, what we would like in our lives, what we would like to change, and so on?

Writing is cathartic and takes place in your subconscious mind. It helps you purge your innermost thoughts and emotions in a safe space. Verbalising your feelings make you look at them from a unique perspective. It is also about taking the time to get to know and observe yourself. This helps develop a sense of self-awareness and enables you to look at areas to improve and areas you can enhance. It helps you reconnect with your inner being and stay focused on the present. It also gives you the space to ideate and formulate steps to achieve your goals and dreams. As a habitual practice, it is a therapy in itself.

Journaling also helps with anxiety and depression. It helps to unload the repetitive thoughts that loop in your mind and makes space for you to fill it with more positive thoughts.

What if someone reads my journal?

I have had many clients express this fear that someone may read their journal, which stops them from writing. While it is a valid fear, it is also used as an excuse. I often ask women if they possess expensive jewellery. Does the fear of the jewellery be stolen keep you from buying it? No, not really. You find a safe spot to house it. The same goes for your journal. You don't need to advertise or draw attention to your journaling practice. You can do it when you find quiet, alone time. There is also the fear of putting one's innermost thoughts and emotions out because, far from the recesses of the safety of one's mind, once it is put out on paper, it becomes real.

Alternatively, would you invade someone else's privacy if you were privy to a journal? Your answer will tell you if that is why you fear someone else reading yours. What we give out is what we get back.

I first started keeping a journal when I was about 12 years old. I was looking to lock my drawers and couldn't find the key to the old writing desk I used. My mother told me to trust her that she would not read it. So, I started writing in code in case anyone was tempted to. But I did keep it hidden in my drawers. Not once did I suspect my mother of reading it, as she never said or acted differently to suggest that either of my parents or siblings had knowledge of anything I might have written. I realise now that my family had healthy boundaries on personal privacy. And thankfully that has continued in my family with my children. I bought them diaries when they were young and taught them to start a gratitude journal. I also explained to them that they could use it to vent if needed, and it would be safe and their privacy respected. And I can say with certainty that I never broke their trust, nor have they mine, as my journal is not locked away. Nor do we peek into each other's phones. We have healthy boundaries, communicate well, and are secure knowing we can approach each other, whatever the problem. So, setting healthy boundaries and inculcating a safe, respectful environment is also necessary.

You can have an online journal on your computer, iPad, or phone as well and have it password protected. However, there is a more direct connection with your subconscious mind when you handwrite in a journal.

What are the various ways of Journaling?

Free writing is simply expressing whatever is on your mind or about your day — expressing your thoughts, feelings, and concerns about your present situation. In this method, there are no boundaries of time or space. You are free to express all that you want to.

Day Planner: You can use the journal to plan your day. This is done in the morning. List your tasks for the day in the order of priority. List three things that you would like to get done for the day. If they are complex tasks, you can spend some time on how you plan to action those tasks.

Dream Journal: this is the practice of recording memories of your dreams as soon as you wake up. Dreams process our emotions and experiences of the day. Dreams are valuable in gaining self-awareness. They help us understand our deepest fears, hopes, and dreams. By paying attention to our dreams, we can discover our shadow self or the parts we do not want to look at consciously. They can also guide and direct us in our lives by showing us alternate ways to communicate, resolve issues and let go of old resentments

Gratitude Journal: This is one of the most effective ways to journal that I advocate and encourage all my clients to do. The gratitude journal encourages you to develop a positive mindset, no matter what you are going through. It is most beneficial if done twice daily. First thing in the morning where you start by writing down five things you are grateful for. It then sets the tone for the day and enables you to establish a positive mindset every day. And the last thing you do before sleeping is to write another five things for what you are grateful for. You can start

with five things but go onto as many that come to mind. The more you realise you have to be thankful for, the less you worry about the problems in your life. This is a highly effective way to cultivate a positive mindset.
There are other ways to journal. You can use journal prompts.

Journal prompts are a framework of questions that can guide you on what areas you want to focus on. Eg.: Where do you see yourself in 5 years? What do you need to change to get there? You can also create vision boards in your journal by drawing or sticking pictures of the things you want to manifest. You can write affirmations as many times as you need to.

What do I need to do to start the practice of journaling?

Buy a lovely journal. Take your time to pick a nice one that resonates with you. Your journal will be your personal space where you share intimate thoughts, so pick something that speaks to you. Buy a couple of your favourite-coloured pens.

Pick out a suitable time for you in the day when you can spend some alone time and be undisturbed.

Make it a daily practice. Write as much as you feel like. There are no rules and no judgement. No one is monitoring you, nor do you need to monitor yourself. The more you open up and release, the greater you will benefit from it. You can doodle, draw, stick pictures in it, or do whatever you like.

Whatever you write, whether to vent or be reflective, at the end of it, I suggest you write your five or more gratitude lists. It helps to always end on a positive note so that you release the negative emotions first and focus on the good already prevalent in your life.

THE EBB AND FLOW IN LIFE

The ebb and flow of the deep blue sea
is the same as it is for you and me.
Sometimes we're at peace with tranquillity.
When life seems to move and lets us be
soothed by the rhythms that keeps us quiet
giving what we need to beautify it.

Sometimes we're turbulent as the stormy sea
wondering how troublesome times can be
upon us so fast, destroying harmony.
And nothing we do keeps us free
as we rock back and forth and to and fro
like strong winds from the north that won't let go.

And finally we learn to accept the change
of the ebb and flow and we rearrange
our thinking and the drift and debris
that comes to us like the sand at the sea.
For this is the natural order of things
that comes to all be they paupers or Kings.

~

by Edwina Reizer

CHAPTER 11

FIND YOUR TRIBE

Your vibe attracts your tribe.

FIND YOUR TRIBE

What does it mean to find your tribe?

Being with people who get you for who you are and having authentic, meaningful relationships with people who love and accept you for who you are. These people respect, support, and elevate you to be the best version of yourself. True friends will support you and be there for you when needed. They will understand you and accept you with all your quirks. They will be honest with you and encourage and motivate you to do your best. Most importantly, they will not judge you for who you are.

These are not your people:

There are always people who will put you down, take advantage of your goodness and kindness, disrespect your views & ideas, and make you feel less than. They are not your tribe. Recognize the patterns of behaviour of others towards you. Learn from experiences. Do not offer up yourself for more humiliation or ridicule by these people. Be friendly, but do not pour your heart out to them. The less you discuss your plans with such people, the better you will be. Some people can be jealous. It takes an unhappy person to feel good about taking another person down. Limit your interactions with such people. Keep the conversations superficial, engage in social banter, but keep the things close to your heart for your real friends.

Tribes may change over time:

Often through life, we outgrow old friendships. It doesn't mean there is any ill feeling. As you evolve and grow, you move forward and may not connect the way you once did. Change is constant. Your friend circle often changes when you get married, divorced, or relocate. You may connect more with young parents like yourself when you have kids. When you hit middle age and find the time to reconnect with yourself, you may outgrow some of your friends and find a new tribe. There is nothing wrong with that. Everyone grows and changes constantly in a lifetime, and whatever stage you are at, you will find new friends that connect with you at that particular time in your life.

Be around people who uplift your soul.

How do I find my tribe?

Be yourself: When you are authentic, honest, and open, you will find like-minded people. What you give out, you get back. Relationships will develop organically if you are yourself, listen to what others say, and accept others for who they are without judgement. Putting yourself out there might be daunting at first, but the benefits of true friendship far outweigh your fears.

Follow your passions: You will meet similar people when you follow your desires and get involved in related activities. By stepping out of your comfort zone and being open to trying out new things, you will meet people who share common interests that bring you together and form special bonds of friendship. E.g., Joining a class, singing in a chorus, playing a sport, or volunteering for a cause.

Be open and adventurous to trying out new things. These interests can be based on different or similar characteristics, ranging from race, gender, and nationality to academic qualifications, occupations, and other attractions.

Be reciprocal. There is give and take in every relationship. Take the initiative to decide if you feel you have a connection with someone. Don't always wait to be invited.

What are the Benefits of Finding My Tribe?

Humans are social and need a sense of belonging.

The tribe we choose
best supports our success and gives
us a sense of belonging, legitimacy,
and self-esteem.

It is representative of shared values, beliefs, activities,
aspirations, and interests.

A tribe or community makes you feel supported,
nurtured, and fulfilled.

Section 2

In this section, I would like to talk about the benefits of finding and living from your true self and connecting with more than just yourself.

Chapter 12

BEING ALIGNED IN THE FLOW OF LIFE

When you do things from your soul,
you feel a river moving in you, a joy.

Rumi

These are two different concepts: being in the flow of one's life and being in the flow state. I am going to talk about both here, as they are both relevant and happen when you start to align all parts of yourself.

What does it mean to be in alignment or the flow of life?

To be in alignment is to be one in body, mind, and soul and connect to your spiritual self or intuition. Mindfulness or living in the present moment enables you to get into the flow of life. Leaving the past behind, clearing negative emotions, and being whole and complete in the present moment and not living in the future either.

When your operating system runs in a state of alignment, you honour who you are and your purpose. You get an inner knowing of how to move forward. Being in the flow also brings a quiet calmness and immense trust in yourself and your higher power to guide you. You learn to live in gratitude for every experience that led you to where you are; however painful the experiences have been. You recognise the lessons and what they came to teach you and move forward with a peaceful contentment of just being a more evolved, learned and wiser you.

Clarity lights up your path once you start to believe and have faith in yourself and your capabilities. You become calm and confident in making the right decisions. To those who believe and have faith in a Higher Power, God, Creator, or Source, you realise you are guided and protected throughout and especially through adversity.

And when you feel that alignment of Mind, Body, and Soul, you understand there are no coincidences. What is meant for you will never pass you by. The lessons we learn, the joys, the sorrows, the wins, and the losses are all that we were meant to experience to teach us and make us more whole. You can only be in control of your mind and not much else. It is up to you and the choices you make. You can approach adversities with courage and grace or with fear and frustration, which makes all the difference. Instead of making a molehill a mountain, it is easier to make the mountain a molehill. It's much easier to scale and climb over. By this I mean, making yourself bigger than the problem and digging deep within to overcome it than to let it bury you. And sometimes, the mountain cannot be perceived as a molehill and that is okay. It is then that we need to remind ourselves that a mountain needs to be scaled one step at a time and not carried as a heavy burden. By now, you know that worry does not change the outcome and is a waste of energy. It takes the flow out of you.

What does it mean to be in the flow state?

When you singularly focus your attention on an activity or task that you feel incredibly passionate about and immerse yourself entirely in it, you can create the conditions necessary to experience a flow state of mind.

When you are in the flow state, you get so absorbed and consumed by performing the activity that you lose track of yourself and the passing of time and are oblivious to your surroundings. You have absolute clarity, a rush of joy, excitement, and knowing how to navigate the task effortlessly. You become one with the job at hand. It is also called being in the 'zone'.

Flow happens when inspired action, and conscious awareness meld together to create an effortless, charged momentum that is joyful and satisfying.

Examples of being in the flow state: *A sports person before and during an event. Eg., Formula1 drivers, swimmers, athletes. An artist, sculptor, painter, or musician at work. Surgeons while operating and chess players contemplating their next move.*

How do I get into the Flow State?

You've got to be a 'Man with a plan'. You need to be passionate about the activity or task. In the words of the famous author Napolean Hill, you must have a 'burning desire'. You will need to set a goal of what you want to achieve and plan how you can get there. Then comes exercising your willpower to start with small steps that lead up to your goal. It will increase your confidence and skill. Once you build the confidence and skill to take on a challenge, you decide and commit to it. It is a crucial step to hold yourself accountable for it. Meditate on it and journal about it. Be excited about it. A small amount of nervousness is good. Most importantly, believe you have the skills and capability to achieve it. Visualise the outcome you would like and then go for it.

Deciding to write this book on a topic I have been passionate about for almost six years now is the perfect example to give you, along with the process I have followed. Writing this book seemed daunting as I was looking for perfection and hesitated to start. However, I did start by writing blogs on the same topics that are my chapters here, in much more detail. Once you decide and commit to it, you meet the right people, your tribe, who encourage, motivate, and teach you how to get closer to achieving your goal. Next, you tap into your inner strength, take a leap of faith, and rise to the challenge. And ever since I started writing this book, the ideas have flowed to me, the resources have revealed themselves to me, and it reiterates that what you focus on, you attract and manifest and you get an immense joy and satisfaction in finally achieving a goal. I was initially nervous and dragged my feet for a couple of days before I started writing my first chapter, and as I sat down, I realised how much information I had collated over the years on this topic and how much thought I had put into it. The writing came with such a cheerful optimism that it flowed through me with ease. At that moment, I knew I was meant to write it, and the rest flowed just as easily and joyfully. From deciding to write the book, the entire process has been in a flow state. I allotted myself a specific time every evening. I looked forward to it. I researched whenever I had free time during the day and gave myself a goal of writing one chapter a day. I was able to complete the book in less than 15 days. Even my friends, who I asked to edit and design the cover, said yes instantly and were happy to do it for me unconditionally.

Being in the flow state is not just about being immersed in the task itself; it happens when you decide to take a leap of faith, tap into your inner being, and realise your potential to be more than you thought possible.

The lyrics of **"One Moment in Time" sung by Whitney Houston** – written by Albert Hammond and John Bettis, have been a prayer, kept me going through tough times, and have shaped my choices through life to strive to be a better version of myself. It is indeed a full circle moment for me, which beautifully elucidates what it means to know "who I am" and to be in flow with the Universe. No matter how this book is received, it will still be my moment in time when I'm more than I ever thought I could be. And I am sure you dear readers, have many such moments in your lives.

Chapter 13

Inter Connectedness

Love reminds us that we are all interconnected,
and it begins with being fully connected to the wisdom, grace,
and divinity of our own being.

Dr. Debra Reble

NO MAN IS AN ISLAND

No man is an island entire of itself; every man
is a piece of the continent, a part of the main;
if a clod be washed away by the sea, Europe
is the less, as well as if a promontory were, as
well as any manner of thy friends or of thine
own were; any man's death diminishes me,
because I am involved in mankind.
And therefore never send to know for whom
the bell tolls; it tolls for thee.

by John Donne

When you get to know your true self, you become aware of the impact your actions have on the whole. You start to realise that we are all interconnected and that each of us has a purpose. The closer we reach our true selves, the closer we reach our purpose.

According to the philosophical and spiritual concept of interconnectedness, all things are interconnected, including nature, our own experiences, and the Universe. We learn from the concept of interconnectedness that we are not isolated individuals but rather a piece of a larger whole. This knowledge profoundly affects our sense of ourselves and how we interact with the world.

In the spiritual world, it is believed that we are interconnected through collective consciousness in nature and humanity. It translates to 'what we put out we get back.' It goes beyond our awareness, where every action, thought, and deed has a bearing and a consequence that ripples down to various levels and affects us and others.

"We cannot live only for ourselves. A thousand fibres connect us with our fellow men, and among those fibres, as sympathetic threads, our actions run as causes, and they come back to us as effects."

~

Herman Melville

I will give you a simple example here of baking a cake. To make the cake, you need to buy ingredients as per the recipe you follow, then focus on making it, baking it, and deciding to decorate it. Once the cake is made, you share it with family or friends, depending.

When you buy the ingredients, you give the store business, the distributors, suppliers, and even the farmers for the flour, cocoa, sugar, eggs, and more. You support various industries just by making a cake. Once you make a cake and are happy with the outcome, you share that happiness with your friends and family. That creates a happy memory, and that joy trickles into their lives for a moment. Making the cake may inspire someone else to bake a cake of their own, find their confidence and spread their confidence and satisfaction to others. Just as the person whose recipe you followed evoked some happy memory and inspired you to recreate it. This is how interconnectedness works. We may not stop to think of how our actions have consequences, but they do.

The movie "Babel" comes to my mind as an excellent example of interconnectedness. If you haven't seen it or watched it recently, I suggest you watch it to understand what I am talking about here. The gist is how one unconscious act in a part of the world affects the lives of a group of people by causing a chain of reactions in different countries around the globe.

"There is a deep interconnectedness of all life on earth,
from the tiniest organism to the largest ecosystems,
and absolutely between each person."

~

Bryant McGill.

We all play a part in a larger whole, and our actions have consequences. If we remain wounded beings and live in our negative emotions, and we can now realize that those emotions, fears, and beliefs trickle down in all our interactions, especially with our children, relationships, and at work. We do have a choice to overcome our fears, change our beliefs and become conscious beings. This journey of evolution, un-becoming who we once were, finding our inner beings, and shining our inner light, helps us lead lives with purpose and awareness. It enables us to leave a more positive footprint behind us that may inspire others to do better and be better by doing it for ourselves.

When you live in fear, insecurities, jealousy, envy, entitlement, greed, and anger, you pull each other down. You do not help each other up. It is because you are unable to recognise your own values and gifts. When you see others break barriers and achieve goals, it irks you, as you too want to be successful; you too wish to have the things that they have achieved, but don't want to make an effort, don't want to step out of your comfort zone, don't want to face your fears and let go of limiting beliefs. Some are already achievers but get threatened by a new achiever who becomes competitive. Once again, this comes from fear and ego. So, you pull them down to where you are by gossiping about them or being mean or nasty to them. Aim to be an achiever, who has compassion and empathy for yourself and your struggles and is secure with who you are and where you are, and you will have the same for someone else. You will support them by cheering them on, giving them advice when asked, and lending a hand when needed. This will make you an evolved, confident being who has faith and trust in him or herself to know that we must all grow, develop, and help those around us. This is the light within you that spreads.

"Love reminds us that we are all interconnected,
and it begins with being fully connected to the wisdom, grace,
and divinity of our own being."
~
Dr. Debra Reble

I received the analogy of pixels in meditation. Imagine that each of us is a pixel that makes up an image. When all the pixels light up, we see the whole image. Imagine, if half the pixels didn't light up, would the image be complete? The same is true for a firework display. Each of those dots of light, called stars, make up the pattern for the display. If some of these stars didn't light up, we wouldn't witness such a spectacular display now, would we? Just like these pixels and stars, we, too, play a part to shine and help others shine, contributing to a more significant whole being more beautiful.

In the words of Archbishop Desmond Tutu- "One of the sayings in our country is Ubuntu - the essence of being human. Ubuntu speaks particularly about the fact that you can't exist as a human being in isolation. It speaks about our interconnectedness. You can't be human all by yourself, and when you have this quality - Ubuntu - you are known for your generosity. We think of ourselves far too frequently as just individuals, separated from one another, whereas you are connected, and what you do affects the whole world. When you do well, it spreads out; it is for the whole of humanity."

The concept of Ubuntu is, "I am because we are."

"In certain regions of South Africa, when someone does something wrong, he/she is taken to the center of the village, and for two days, he/she is surrounded by his tribe, while they speak of all the good, he/she has done. They believe that each person is good yet sometimes we make mistakes, which is really a cry for help. They unite in this ritual to encourage the person to reconnect with his true nature. The belief is that unity and affirmation have more power to change behaviour than does shame and punishment. This is known as Ubuntu – humanity towards others." – Kristine Dewar on the Meaning of Ubuntu.

CHAPTER 14

THE JOYS OF LIVING FROM YOUR AUTHENTIC SELF

The authentic self is the soul made visible.

~

Sarah Ban Breathnach

The Joys of Living from your Authentic Self.

As you live from your authentic self, you feel more connected spiritually and to all around you. You can relate to others with love and empathy rather than judgement. You start to see signs and synchronicities and can connect the dots when you look back; you see how things fell into place. The feeling is beautiful and blissful.

When you allow yourself to be whole and complete, you find a deeper meaning within, what you want your life to be and how you want to live your life. Connecting to the voice within you guides you, and you can live with clarity and focus. That inner voice is your intuition. Your intuition is your 'gut feeling,' also called a 'sixth sense.' That is the voice of your higher being, your soul, and your true self. Only when you decide to change, take action, and persist will you see changes in your life.

Have you ever had the experience of when you did something to step out of your comfort zone, when you somehow overcame the resistance and went to an event or meeting or did something unusual? When you did something like that, did it open new pathways for you? For instance, meeting the love of your life, meeting a future business associate, or finding someone to help you resolve a long-standing issue? I am sure you all can recall some moment that changed your life tremendously when you followed your inner voice. That is your intuition that guides us through life, and if only listen to it more intently, while silencing your mind and ego, life becomes smoother and easier- 'to row that boat, gently down the stream.'

When you allow your authentic self to be present, to accompany you in your daily life, You will find you have more clarity, You have a knowing of how to navigate your day, You find bliss in the smallest of things, You make gratitude a part of your daily living.

You start to see beyond your ego, you will be able to see that someone being nasty or mean must be in pain or have an issue to behave in that manner.

Sometimes you need to be firm and stand up for things you feel strongly about, and you do so with conviction.

You have no need to interfere in others' lives or pass judgement.
There is no guilt or second-guessing yourself.

It is then that you know you are one with yourself.

Being in control of our emotions, having clarity on how much we can give and balancing out our lives to be calm and secure with who we are, comes from our authenticity. While we play separate roles in our lives, that of a spouse, parent, child, employer, employee and many more, we bring various facets of ourselves in each of these roles. They are all a part of us. Authenticity is bringing your true unconditional self into every one of these roles.

Signs and Synchronicities.

When you align more with who you truly are and feel more whole and complete, you start seeing signs and synchronicities from the Universe. You can also ask for signs.

I asked for a white downy feather, as I am not too fond of large feathers. I've had some incidents with birds that have scarred me a bit. Not long after asking for the feathers, I saw a cloud shaped like a giant fluffy feather in the sky on my walk one evening. On a walk, my path home is always sporadically lined with soft downy feathers.

Sometimes you will hear songs with a special meaning play unexpectedly on the radio. Whenever I've had a problem to solve and asked for guidance, I get a song with lyrics that somehow show me the path I should take or a confirmation of what I have been thinking about.

The Universe has a great sense of humour. E.g. I love playing the lottery and sometimes, before a big jackpot, I keep hoping to win. When I get into the car, the radio comes on, and "I Wanna Be a Billionaire" by Travie Mccoy starts to play. It makes me laugh because that has been exactly on my mind. While I haven't had a lottery win yet, it is reassuring to know that I am being heard somewhere out there in the vast cosmos.

Then of course there is also telepathy. Sometimes you will have the urge to call on someone, and when you do the person tells you that they have been thinking of calling you. And the more you get aligned, you realise that when you have a strong urge to call someone and you do, invariably the person may be going through some tough time and may have needed that call.

As you get more aligned, you can also see repetitive numbers, **Eg.: 111, 222, 333.** These are called angel numbers. When you ask for signs, you start to see them. The way to get there is to believe that you will. It took me a while and I see them all the time now. Different numbers have different meanings, but most importantly, it makes you feel like you are not alone. It makes you feel like the Universe hears you and has your back. The intention is not for you to feel pressured that you don't see them and make you feel less than, it is just a matter of time and getting into the frequency to be able to experience it.

"This is called Synchronicity,
a state in which you almost feel as if you are
already in a collaborative arrangement with fate"
~
Wayne Dyer

There are times when you feel that things are not going according to plan and you may fret or get frustrated. Remember to take a step back, chances are you might be put in a situation to protect you from something worse happening. E.g., If you are having a series of unfortunate events on a particular morning where you can't find your keys, spill coffee on your clothes, and are forced to leave home later than usual. Then you get onto the road in your vehicle, only to be diverted because of an accident on your regular route. If you stop to think, if you had been on time, you most likely would have been involved in the accident as it occurred at the same time you might have customarily crossed that spot? This is an example of how guidance works.

Sometimes accidents do happen, or tragedy does strike. While we struggle to comprehend it, it makes us find strength within to help us overcome the situation. It also changes our trajectory, our perceptions and our lives.

'If only one thing had happened differently, but life being what it is - a series of intersecting lives and incidents, out of anyone's control' ~ Eric Roth. (The Curious Case of Benjamin Button). Please watch the accident scene in the movie or on YouTube to understand this better.

SUMMARY

The purpose of this book is to help you look within and find who you are after peeling off layers of conditioning, the roles you play, and to simply find your essence, your song, your being. It is a process of unbecoming, to be the real you and who you would like to be. This changes with time and experiences, where you let go of all that does not serve you any longer and embrace the parts you want, to feel one with yourself. In doing so, you align with the Universe and are able to play your part harmoniously as one in the greater scheme of things.

Think of your feelings when you see a new born baby or cuddle and play with a pet. There are sounds like cooing and aahing, which comes from a sense of innate love and joy. There are no thoughts, words or judgment; it is pure emotion. You experience unconditional love, which is who you are at your core before conditioning and ego took over.

I think of myself and my fellow beings as 'mosaics.' We are all fragmented bits and pieces put together as a whole that makes up a beautiful picture. It is the acceptance, healing and amalgamation of all the broken, frayed, torn parts of ourselves, woven together with all our strength and courage that makes us unique and beautiful. The awareness and effort we put in to embracing our flaws and imperfections with love and acceptance, make us whole and complete. When we do that for ourselves, we show our authenticity and uniqueness, which brings beauty and inspiration to others, much like the Japanese' Kintsugi.'- The art of mending broken pottery.

To summarize, I am going to share a beautiful excerpt from the legendary poet **Herman Hesse** which encapsulates all I have tried to convey in this book.

"For me, trees have always been the most penetrating preachers. I revere them when they live in tribes and families, in forests and groves. And even more I revere them when they stand alone. They are like lonely persons. Not like hermits who have stolen away out of some weakness, but like great, solitary men, like Beethoven and Nietzsche. In their highest boughs the world rustles, their roots rest in infinity; but they do not lose themselves there, they struggle with all the force of their lives for one thing only: to fulfil themselves according to their own laws, to build up their own form, to represent themselves. Nothing is holier, nothing is more exemplary than a beautiful, strong tree. When a tree is cut down and reveals its naked death-wound to the sun, one can read its whole history in the luminous, inscribed disk of its trunk: in the rings of its years, its scars, all the struggle, all the suffering, all the sickness, all the happiness and prosperity stand truly written, the narrow years and the luxurious years, the attacks withstood, the storms endured. And every young farm boy knows that the hardest and noblest wood has the narrowest rings, that high on the mountains and in continuing danger the most indestructible, the strongest, the ideal trees grow.

A tree says:

A kernel is hidden in me, a spark, a thought, I am life from eternal life. The attempt and the risk that the eternal mother took with me is unique, unique the form and veins of my skin, unique the smallest play of leaves in my branches and the smallest scar on my bark. I was made to form and reveal the eternal in my smallest special detail.

A tree says:

My strength is trust. I know nothing about my fathers, I know nothing about the thousand children that every year spring out of me. I live out the secret of my seed to the very end, and I care for nothing else. I trust that God is in me. I trust that my labour is holy. Out of this trust I live.

When we are stricken and cannot bear our lives any longer, then a tree has something to say to us:

Be still! Be still! Look at me! Life is not easy; life is not difficult. Those are childish thoughts. Let God speak within you, and your thoughts will grow silent. You are anxious because your path leads away from mother and home. But every step and every day lead you back again to the mother. Home is neither here nor there. Home is within you, or home is nowhere at all.

A longing to wander tears my heart when I hear trees rustling in the wind at evening. If one listens to them silently for a long time, this longing reveals its kernel, its meaning. It is not so much a matter of escaping from one's suffering, though it may seem to be so. It is a longing for home, for a memory of the mother, for new metaphors for life. It leads home. Every path leads homeward, every step is birth, every step is death, every grave is mother.

So the tree rustles in the evening, when we stand uneasy before our own childish thoughts:
Trees have long thoughts, long-breathing and restful, just as they have longer lives than ours. They are wiser than we are, as long as we do not listen to them. But when we have learned how to listen to trees, then the brevity and the quickness and the childlike hastiness of our thoughts achieve an incomparable joy. Whoever has learned how to listen to trees no longer wants to be a tree. He wants to be nothing except what he is. That is home. That is happiness."

~

Herman Hesse
Bäume: Betrachtungen und Gedichte

My thoughts...

scribble. express. doodle. write. draw. get creative.

My thoughts...

scribble. express. doodle. write. draw. get creative.

My thoughts...

My thoughts...

My thoughts...

scribble. express. doodle. write. draw. get creative.

My thoughts...

scribble. express. doodle. write.draw. get creative.

My thoughts...

scribble. express. doodle. write. draw. get creative.

My thoughts...

scribble. express. doodle. write. draw. get creative.

My thoughts...